GIRLS ABOVE SOCIETY

Steps to Success:
An Empowerment Guide

A Young Girl's Guide to Believing in Herself
and Following Her Dreams ~

Lauren Galley

www.girlsabovesociety.org

GIRLS ABOVE SOCIETY

STEPS TO SUCCESS: AN EMPOWERMENT GUIDE

copyright@ 2013

By Lauren Marie Galley

Edited by Tina Cafeo

Cover Art by Kayti Welsh
www.kaytidesigns.com

ISBN-13:
978-0615834887 (Girls Above Society)
ISBN-10:
0615834884

Contact Information: girlsabovesociety@att.net
visit us at www.girlsabovesociety.org

Printed in The United States of America

DEDICATION

I would love to dedicate this book to my mom, who has been by my side, through the good times and the bad and who has always given me with unconditional love, wise guidance and support. I am reaching all of my goals and achieving all my successes due to her and my father's strength and ability to let me fly and follow the path that I have chosen... yet, I know they are there to catch me if I fall. This gives me the power to soar and I love, admire and respect them for being such wonderful parents. They have taught me compassion, love and respect... all the qualities I choose to live by today. One of my main goals in writing this book, is to honor my mom. She is my best friend in the entire world and always will be!

THANK YOU

Having friends that stick beside you no matter what, that go through the good and bad times with you, are so important. I have learned that having best friends is not always quantity, it's quality. I would like to thank MY best friends for their never ending support and encouragement to make a difference.

Nicole Parker – Where do I even begin? You have been there for me literally since day one. I am so proud to call you my best friend! We have been through so much together and our friendship has never faltered, if anything it grows everyday. Your strength and courage that you possess for life is truly inspiring and it motivates me to fearlessly face life head-on. I wake up every morning confident that you truly care about me. That is the true definition of a best friend. THANK YOU for making my life so amazing!

Meagan Parker – I am so grateful to have you in my life. You are always such a huge support system for me. I know in my heart that you genuinely mean all the kind words you say to me and it makes me so happy to know I have someone so amazing to encourage me through life. You are such an easy and fun person to be around. There is never any drama or stress, just lots of laughs and smiles. I will always be there for you, never forget that!

Meghan Menasco– You are one of the funniest people I know! I genuinely mean that. There is never a dull moment when we are together. We have that kind of friendship where we can literally talk about anything and it's not "weird" or "awkward." You are such a great friend and one of the most caring people that I know. You care about your friends more than yourself and I love that about you. I can't wait to see where our lives take us next, but I know we will be together through it all!

CONTENTS

FOREWORD

by Braxton A. Cosby

Award Winning Author of *Protostar: The Star-Crossed Saga* and the upcoming new series *The School of Ministry: The Windgate*

What is it like to be a young girl in this age? Or a woman for that matter? The times are changing, at a rapid pace, insomuch that gender roles have shifted, identities have been blurred and moral standard bars have been lowered, if not completely removed. Our young people are the victims. The have become slaves of depravity and debauched ways of thinking, that make them feel inept, insecure and self-conscious. They now have to run to television, music and celebrity idols for guidance, where more times than not the cycle just repeats itself. Parenting has become a battle of attrition in a tug-o-war of us against these piling factors. In this war, the floodwaters of confusion and anxiety have crashed against the precious minds of the future.

Being a father of three girls, I for one have drawn my line in the sand and prepared myself for a battle that will most likely last a lifetime. I know where my strength comes from, but where are our children turning for encouragement? Well finally, a book has come along that offers a flicker of hope and lends a voice to the youth of our age that will inspire, encourage, and reunite this era with the moral baselines of the past. That voice has come in the form of Miss Lauren Galley.

Steps To Success: An Empowerment Guide is a book that shifts the tide and sets sail in the right direction. Each chapter offers a nugget that young girls can grasp and utilize to empower themselves in dealing with the day-to-day struggles of the current time. The simple, easy to read, practical, matter-o-fact language that Lauren uses will speak not only to the heart, but of the minds of young girls everywhere. Lauren has used her voice to speak to girls all over the nation and has now encapsulated the pureness of her messaging in between these pages, so that girls can have it at their fingertips. Anyone who reads *Steps To Success: An Empowerment Guide* will find some takeaway point that resonates with their past experiences of growing up (older folks like me), and lay a foundation for the inevitable trials of the future (younger folks).

Thank you Lauren for your hard work and dedication to messaging confidence and your commitment to leadership in a generation starving for voices that promote positive change. I enjoyed reading this book and I know that readers will also.

Enjoy!

ACKNOWLEDGMENTS

I feel completely blessed and honored to have so many wonderful mentors guiding me through this amazing journey. Being able to put my words and vision on these pages represents a milestone in my life. The idea of having girls throughout the world read this book is a dream come true. I would like to acknowledge some incredibly important individuals who have made a difference in my life and have contributed in one way or another to my thought process in creating this book.

Kayti Welsh is one of the most creative and visual graphic artists that I know and I am so privileged to have her create my website and be such a huge part of the drawings and graphics that you see in this book. Not only is she talented, but she is a genuine and giving human being and I am so happy to call her my friend.

Cylk Cozart is not only my mentor, but one of the most talented actors I have ever seen on screen. He has been there for me since the day I had the idea of Girls Above Society and he continues to be there and support me one hundred percent.

Michelle Phillips is one big dose of girl power and I feel so fortunate to work with her. Her support and encouragement reminds me daily that I can do anything! The Beauty Blueprint, by Michelle Phillips, is changing my life and provided inspiration for this guide.

I could not have self-published this book with the ease that I have without the help of Merel Bakker, author of Maks & Mila. She is one of the most giving and caring people on this Earth.

Authors Marianne de Pierres and Braxton Cosby are not only amazing writers, but continue to support youth. They are selfless mentors that encourage me to fly.

Last, but most certainly not least, this book would not have been possible without the editing assistance of Tina Cafeo. I never had grandparents growing up and I am proud to say I consider her the Grandma I never had.

INTRODUCTION

I wrote this book in my own words for all the teen girls out there going through the tough pressures of today's media driven society. Being a teenager myself, it wasn't that long ago that I was in middle school and high school. I still relate to those pressures as I continue to face them today.

More than 90 percent of girls – 15 to 17 years – want to change at least one aspect of their physical appearance, with body weight ranking the highest.

80% of children who are 10 years old are afraid of being fat.

7 in 10 girls believe they are not good enough or do not measure up in some way including their looks, performance in school and relationships.

My hopes are that you read my book and put my steps in place as you grow into a confident, driven Girl Above Society! I'm wishing you much success in finding your "sparkle" and taking your Girl Power to the Extreme!

XOXO *Lauren*

SOURCES:
HEART OF LEADERSHIP
DOVE CAMPAIGN FOR REAL BEAUTY
PBS

WHO AM I?

Who am I? A question all of us ponder many times throughout our pre-teen and teen years. Even into their twenties, young people are always trying to set their place in an extremely demanding, judgmental society, racked with expectations and filled with harmful temptations. OMG! That's scary. How is a young girl supposed to successfully navigate these waters? You ask yourself, "How am I going to fit into all of this? Where is my place?" Many young girls do not have a clue about these questions. I hope by the time you finish reading my book, you will have answers and a positive game plan.

Somehow, many girls muddle through life, simply hoping they will somehow figure out what they want to do with their lives. Don't be so lazy. Take charge of your life... you only have "one." Don't just be content with finishing school, a mediocre job, then marriage and children. There is a spot in there you need to fill. Decide what you are passionate about, become an expert in the field and create a successful career for yourself. You're lucky! This is a much different world than the one your grandmother lived in... women back then were not encouraged to reach their full potential. The only expectations most parents had, were that their kids grew up, got married and the wife was a stay at home mom who cleaned the house, canned vegetables and prepared meals. She took care of her kids' needs, and did what her husband, "the bread winner," told her. YUCK!

Good news...this is the 21st Century and you are free to do what you choose. Be a doctor or the President of the United States. THINK BIG!

All of us are so fortunate because today's young women have every opportunity in the world open to them. You can determine your own success, depending on how hard you are willing to work and what sacrifices you will make.

Let's create a motto. "I will reach my fullest potential. I will become a Girl Above Society! One who knows who she is, where she is going and what she is going to be!"

So, now we have established the fact THE WORLD IS YOUR OYSTER... OPEN IT UP AND DISCOVER THAT PEARL.

Successfully accomplishing this will take time, patience, dedication, sacrifice and perseverance. Are you up for the challenge? The proceeding steps are what you can take to empower yourself to be who you want and have a fantastic life.

Remember, this is your journey and the ride will be half the fun!

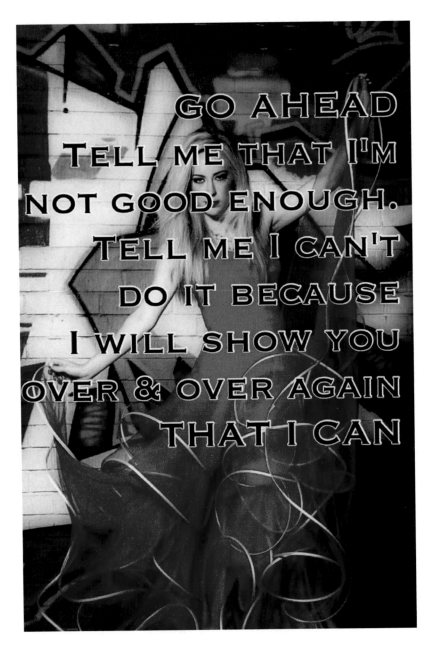

One of my favorite photo shoots from
my photographer Kevin Chappell

STEPS TO SUCCESS

1. Decide who you are and if you don't know, make the effort to think about it very seriously. Ask yourself the "AM I" questions to determine this. They are listed after these 10 steps.

2. Decide what your goals are and what you have to do to reach them. Don't sit around being lazy. Get up and get going... don't stop until you have reached where you want to be. The excitement of your future will energize you!

3. Decide what your values are and what is important to you. Have good morals and stick to them!

4. Prioritize! This is simple. You know what is the most important thing you should concentrate on getting done first. Your homework, for instance or practicing a musical instrument, etc. Even your chores around the house need to be done before you go to a friend's house or shopping at the mall. Believe me, I get it... shopping is important, but not as important. When you are getting your school work and chores done, your parents are happy. Happy parents make for good relations at home. That should be important to you.

5. Work on your relationship with your family and friends.

6. Set up reachable goals for yourself. Reaching them will give you a great deal of satisfaction and the "feel good fuzzies." It will also make you proud of yourself.

7. Learn to have respect for authority. Do not be so immature as to role your eyes at the teacher when she is handing out an assignment. When you start driving, don't text. I shouldn't even have to mention don't drink or do drugs! Rules and the law have a crucial place in society.

8. Find a mentor.

9. Decide if you want to be popular. If so, you will have to learn to successfully juggle time between your interests, your career, your family and friends. Many girls do this very successfully.

10. Understand your relationship with God. Whatever your religion is, if you believe in God, you need to understand and embrace your religious beliefs and respect the beliefs of others, even when they are different than yours

Now, let's dive into the Steps to Success. In order to do this, try looking in the mirror and takng a good look at the face staring back at you. Forget the outer looks, but instead look deep into your eyes and be honest. Ask yourself the "AM I" questions.

A. **Am I confident?** Being the best person you can be begins with confidence. I am sure you have found yourself in a crowded room where there's one person you find yourself admiring. He or she just exudes an air of confidence that you envy. How do you develop this? First of all, get rid of any negative feelings. They will make you feel inferior. Negativity brings you down. Positivity lifts you up. This could be another one of your mottos. Once you have finished reading my book and set goals, this alone should give you a good vibe that will energize you and give you a whole new aura.

B. **Am I loving to my family and friends?** I had to learn that when I'm getting along well with my family, that filters over into my relationships with my friends, teachers and everyone else that I come in contact with. Plus, an important tip. I truly feel you should make your best friends your mother and father. They are the ones who love you the most and will be there to pick you up every time you fall or to console you when you are having a terrible day or problems at school. Their love will never cease or falter. Friends and boyfriends will come and go, but your parents will always be there. Even if they are divorced, you can still have a great relationship with both of them. Your happiness will be directly affected by having a good relationship with your parents.

You will go to school happier and be in better spirits. If things go wrong, you know you have them to turn to, but you must remember one thing... good parents set up rules and boundaries, especially for pre-teens and teens. They do that because they love you and want you safe and headed in a positive direction with your life. They do not do it "to be mean" like some teenagers feel.

Now, if you think a rule is too strict or should be changed, talk to them about it in a nice manner. Don't do it with an "attitude." Parents hate it when their kids get an attitude and that will automatically make them more strict, just when you want them to lighten up, so remember, the way you approach a subject with your parents can make the difference in them understanding your side and then possibly reaching a compromsise. It's all up to you! This also applies to how you relate to your siblings, friends and teachers. A great attitude and approach can make life a lot easier.

C. **Am I communicative?** Do I get my point across in a timely and accurate manner? You need to learn how to talk to your parents, siblings, teachers and friends in a way that they understand exactly what you're saying and what you mean. Teachers are sometimes very difficult to deal with since a lot of them feel they are overworked and underpaid and that e.g.: and they feel that most kids of today have very little respect for authority. You prove them wrong! Be polite and respectful when you go to them with a problem or find yourself failing a class. They will be much more likely to help you if you treat them with respect. NO DRAMA PLEASE! They hate drama. The opposite is true of most of your friends, who probably thrive on gossip and drama, so save it for them if you decide you must act out and a PS to this teacher thing is that if you're doing poorly in class, take charge of the situation right away. It is easier to bring a D up to a B or A, then it is to take the class again in summer school. Talk about your problems when they are small... don't wait until the problem is unfixable.

D. **Am I responsible?** That is something I had to really work on in order to be able to keep up with all my school work and acting in various movies and TV shows, that I was fortunate enough to have come my way. Plus, modeling, participating in various charitable functions and school organizations are very important to me, so what did I have to learn? TIME MANAGEMENT. Juggling all these things really made me sit down and figure a schedule for my entire week. If I had free time, I could spend it with my family, friends or sometimes a boyfriend. I don't have one right now... that stinks, but the older I get, I find myself becoming more particular and selective about who I date. I have dated a lot of frogs and a couple of toads, but... you have to do that to finally find your Prince, so I have high hopes for the future.

Anyway, getting back to managing your time. Get a calendar that you can write in all those little boxes for the various days of the month. Once you write down your schedule, you will find it so much easier to fit in all the extra things you want to do or you may find out you don't have time to do them. Then you have to determine what is important and what comes first and foremost. Also, remember, being responsible means people can count on you to do what you said you would accomplish or to be at work on time if you have a small part-time job after school. Being on time means if you are scheduled to show up at 5:00, you don't get there at 5:05! Be ten or fifteen minutes early as a matter of fact. It makes you look good to your employer.

The two "R's" (responsible and respectful) will earn you a lot of points from the people you deal with and, remember, there is always a time in your life when you need a recommendation for college or a job!

E.   **Am I able to pick myself up, brush myself off and try, try again?** FAILURE IS NOT AN OPTION. Take your goals seriously and remember that thousands of famous people have had many failures before reaching success. That old saying "overnight success" does not exist in most cases. Hard work, perseverance, studying and sacrifices depict today's successful people, so don't let yourself be discouraged when things are not going well or as you planned. Sometimes failure is the best teacher of all!

Failure makes you take stock of yourself and the situation. It can make you try harder just to show everyone and yourself you can do it. Learn from your failures. Never get down on yourself. Have conversations with yourself in your mind and talk yourself out of any depressing thoughts. Listening to music I enjoy helps me or think to yourself, "I Can, I Can."

F.   **Am I Proactive?** I hope so. It will make your life so much easier. Unfortunately, we cannot control everything that happens, so when things don't go well, decide to handle the situation in a positive manner and then the end result will leave everyone feeling good about themselves. For instance, say you misunderstood an assignment in school or just didn't do it, so the teacher gives you an "F." APOLOGIZE. Then make up the work and hand it in to her. If nothing else, it make you appear like a student that really cares and to admit your mistake.

If you do something that upsets your parents and they are yelling at you... instead of getting mad at them because you think they are unjustly nagging on you... apologize and assure them it will not happen again. A little humility goes a long way into making you a better person.

Remember four things: Do not be easily offended, make the best out of a bad situation, don't get angry and figure out how to fix the problem.

G. **Am I kind to others?** Even when they are not kind to you. Sometimes it seems too hard to grit your teeth and bear it, but go ahead... be the better person. It will diffuse a bad situation and make you feel good about yourself.

Most importantly, do **RANDOM ACTS OF KINDNESS FOR OTHERS.** You can't imagine the great deal of positive energy you will feel, until you actually go out of your way to do something very nice for someone less fortunate than you. Try it!

H. **Do not be easily offended.** This is very, very hard for a pre-teen and teenager to do. However, you do not want to be a reactive person. That means you react out of anger and hurt feelings. This would only make the situation worse, so if you have a tendency to be like this, start now to fix this problem. Stop, take some deep breaths, calm yourself down and then handle the situation. As I said before, be Proactive.

I. **You are responsible for making your goals and plans happen.** Yes, others may help you, but you are ultimately the one who needs to make sure that you are headed in the direction you want. One of the rules is "don't get sidetracked." STAY FOCUSED. Don't be afraid of hard work. It makes you a stronger person. It makes you appreciate the final result more.

Another fun photo from Kevin Chappell

BEAUTY IS SKIN DEEP

Remember, I previously suggested you take a deep, honest look in the mirror. Well, that leads me into a discussion on beauty. Being beautiful on the outside is superficial and limited strictly to visual appeal.

So many of us strive to be perfect visually, that we fail to concentrate on the inner beauty, which is so much more important and vital to how we are truly perceived. I blame reality TV and celebrities for this. They create a false sense to pre-teen and teen girls to look and act a certain way. That only rings true when the camera is focused on you and you are being paid to create a character or model down the runway. The world of TV, movies and modeling judges you on outward appearance... yes! However, only a very small percentage of people live in that world.

Your world will expect more and usually lives by the motto beauty is only skin deep. True! Let's add to that... being a loving, compassionate, kind person on the inside will make you a beautiful person on the outside. You will feel so good about yourself you will literally begin to smile more and develop a wonderful personality. People will want to be your friend and they will want to be around you because you make them feel good about themselves and life.

This photo shows the everyday me!
When I'm not at a photo shoot or
filming I wear little to no makeup ~

How often have you seen a beautiful girl or a handsome guy, but they are so obnoxious and self centered that no one really likes them? Don't wear those shoes! If you follow my steps, you will become so popular, focused, successful, kind and likable you won't have time for the huge amount of people who want to be your friend.

Now, after you accomplish developing yourself into such a fabulous person, you can then work on your outer looks because I am not saying makeup and pretty clothes are not important. What I am saying, is that they will never make you into a great person. Makeup and the clothes are the finishing touches. They are simply tools that you use, to help you evolve into the total person you want the world to see. That phrase "total person" is very important.

Once you have implemented my previous steps to success and empowerment, you will become 100% a Girl Above Society. Now, this will take months of practice and patience on your part. Don't let yourself get discouraged. There are many young girls that will not put the time and energy into re-inventing themselves, but believe me... if you make the effort you will reap the rewards.

"Find your inner beauty and sunshine will follow you all day long."

– Lauren Galley

FIND A MENTOR

You need to start figuring out what it is you are passionate about and how that can evolve into a career for you. As a matter of fact, you may already know what you want to do with your life. You can aspire to become anything you want to be in today's world, but achieving that goal will take time, dedication, and discipline. It will mean that there are times you will need to sacrifice doing something you were really looking forward to. There will be nights you will have to be home working on a project or studying, while your friends are out partying.

Welcome to the real world! Achieving success in your chosen profession will most likely mean you will have to attend college. How exciting. College will not only help you gain knowledge and training for your career, it will also help you mature and learn to live on your own, make wise choices and become responsible. It is also a place where you can have some of the best years of your life. There are many exciting activities and clubs to join once you are in a college or university.

You may go a completely different path. Many young women are joining the armed forces and making a career in the army, air force, etc. Many young women are becoming doctors, lawyers or heads of corporations.

Ask yourself a very vital question... WHERE DO YOU SEE YOURSELF IN 15 YEARS? This should help you make a wise choice.

The most important thing is to decide what it is you would love to do to earn a living and be productive. There are so many wonderful opportunities available for young girls today. DREAM BIG!

First though, you need to make the decision about the direction you want to go. Try not to make money a factor in deciding on your career and college. There are so many ways you can get scholarships and aid, so your main concern should be to follow your dreams.

Now, the next step is finding a mentor... someone who has become successful in your chosen profession. Find someone who wants to help young people and is interested in assisting them in developing their talents and education. You need to find someone who has good morals and values that they will encourage and instill in you.

Choose a person who is highly respected in their profession and who demonstrates high standards. A good mentor is someone who will be there to pick you up when you take a fall or dry your tears when things do not go as planned. That person will always encourage you to do the right thing. He or she will lead you in a positive direction.

" Anyone who ever gave you confidence, you owe them a lot."

Kevin Chappell Photography

EXPERIENCE IS THE BEST TEACHER

Let me take the time to relate a rather long experience I had, which I really learned a good lesson from.

I was on the cheer team in middle school and absolutely loved it (at first.) My best friend was on the team with me and most of the other girls seemed really cool. I was a "flyer," so I got to be front and center the majority of the time. This boosted my confidence tremendously.

However, it wasn't long before that all came crashing down. There was a girl on the team named Taylor and she was very "popular." We became very close friends after a few practices. She was dating a boy named Cody, who I had always thought to be very cute and funny. You might even say I had a crush on him. I didn't do anything about it though... mostly because I had a boyfriend who I was crazy about and also because I knew he was dating Taylor, so that wouldn't be fair.

One day, I was innocently walking in the hallway, minding my own business, when Cody walked up to me and said "hey." We had a casual conversation that must have been fairly unmemorable because I'm not sure what it was about. Then, we parted our ways to go to our next classes and forgot about the encounter for the most part. However, that afternoon at cheer practice, I walked into the gym and immediately saw Taylor there doing stretches. I greeted her and asked her about her day and noticed a drastic change in her behavior... she seemed very short with me. I knew I hadn't done anything wrong, so I assumed it to be a bad day for her and continued on with practice.

That night, I was at home on my computer on MySpace (which seems ancient now) and saw what was called a "bulletin" posted by Taylor. This was basically the equivalent to a status on Facebook. I clicked on it, to see what she had to say because the title made me curious.

"Her." Italicized and all. The image is sketched in my memory forever. As I read on, I realized that someone must have really made her angry. I will never forget the words she wrote. The basic idea was that she was backstabbed by some fake girl she thought was a friend and she was warning people to NEVER speak to this girl because she is a bitch, slut and will try to steal your boyfriend in a heartbeat. She also related that this girl's attempts were pathetic saying... I loosely quote... "I'm way hotter than her and there is NO way Cody would EVER be interested in a girl like that."

By this point, I was thinking... oh, this must have been what she was upset about at practice. I felt sorry for her until I read the last line. "Who is the backstabbing bitch, you ask? Why none other than Lauren Galley. That's right! DO NOT TRUST HER. She is a psycho slut."

I couldn't believe the words I had just read. My heart dropped to my stomach and I felt my eyes filling up with angry tears. I had no idea what I had done wrong. I thought we were friends. I was so embarrassed... plus, we lived in a small town, so I knew that by the time school came in the morning, everyone would know about her post. I couldn't face my classmates, especially not Cody or even worse, Taylor, but I knew that my not going to school would give her immense satisfaction, so I sucked it up and went to school.

My day went surprisingly easily and the only people who seemed to know about the post were my best friends and they agreed Taylor was acting crazy, so that encouraged me to ignore it. However, my day wasn't over! The dreaded cheer practice was here and as I took the long way to the gym, I could feel my body almost physically collapsing at the weight of facing her.

I didn't know whether I should confront her, ignore her or what. When I was walking into the gym, she was the first person I saw. Almost as if she was waiting for me, the look on her face told me she was expecting me and she said, loud enough for the whole team to hear, "What the hell are you looking at?" Everyone immediately looked at me and I wasn't sure how to respond. In the literal sense, I really didn't know the proper answer to that. I actually wasn't looking at her on purpose... she was just physically standing in my line of sight.

I awkwardly brushed past her, feeling my face turn what was probably a ridiculous shade of red. I sat in the locker room and told myself I was going to survive this practice and then talk to her in private after practice.

I caught up with her in the hallway and asked if we could talk. She said "I have nothing to say to you." I tried explaining that I wasn't trying to steal Cody from her. I actually thought they were great together. He had just stopped to say hi. "Oh yeah, so it's his fault now, so typical," she retorted back. I couldn't help but noting her eyes tearing up though and she was avoiding my eye contact. Perhaps maybe she wasn't as tough as everyone thought. With that, she stormed away. I avoided her as much as possible after that. Ironically, Cody actually broke up with her a few days later. (Nothing to do with me, of course.)

The rest of the school year was alright, but since it was a small town, I couldn't help but run into her often. We ran with the same group of friends, so it was always uncomfortable and I found it ridiculous that she could make me feel so small and inferior to her, just by being in the same room.

I didn't have to deal with her long because about six months after that I found out we were moving across the country. I was sad because I was going to miss my friends, including Cody. We had become closer friends after their breakup.

The last day of school I had a little going away party in the library, complete with cupcakes, balloons and presents. I remember hugging my friends and tearing up because I would miss them. While I was doing this, I noticed Taylor hovering around the doorway, looking dejected. I excused myself from my friends and walked over to her. There was an uncomfortable silence, then she started crying and reached out to hug me. I was kind of nervous, not knowing if there was a trap or not. My instinct was to just hug her back, so I did. When she calmed down, she said "I'm so sorry, Lauren I can't believe how mean I was to you. I have always been so jealous of you, ever since you moved here and I saw you as a threat. It was the only bad thing I could think of to say about you. I wanted everyone to hate you, which is really stupid. I wasted so much time that we could have been friends. You have no idea how much I regret this and on top of it all, Cody broke up with me because he said I was acting immature and that you're a really nice girl. I'm really sorry. I understand if you hate me and never want to talk to me again."

As much as I wanted to dislike her, I couldn't. I understood where she was coming from. I found myself feeling sorry for her. I had actually always been a little jealous of her beauty, popularity and cute boyfriend. I was silently thrilled that Cody had stood up for me. I told her I didn't hate her and that we would keep in touch. I thanked her for the apology and said I actually thought she was really nice.

This was a huge weight lifted off my shoulders. The Taylor I had liked so much was back and it was a relief.

Several confessions happened that day. Cody confessed that he had always liked me and had actually broken up with Taylor partly because he liked me, but would have anyway since she was acting "crazy." However, I had a boyfriend at the time, so the timing wouldn't have worked out... which is okay, since I believe things happen for a reason.

I still keep in touch with both of them on occasion. Taylor is doing great and learned a big lesson from the whole thing. She is in a happy relationship at this point. Cody is engaged to the love of his life, who I was also friends with in middle school. I couldn't be happier for them. Friends come and go, but the most important thing is that you learn something from the entire experience.

I learned that cyber bullies are probably really insecure themselves and that sometimes all we need is a hug from a friend or words of encouragement and praise. Also, girlfriends, there's no sense in losing friendships over a boy. Neither of us ended up with him and we are both incredibly happy today!

LAUREN GALLEY, PRESIDENT www.girlsabovesociety.org

Kevin Chappell Photography

IS SHE A REAL FRIEND?

Having a real friend is so important to us girls. As you can see from reading the last chapter, sometime people you think are real friends are simply acquaintances because they don't give 100% to the friendship. You may have lots of acquaintances, but your REAL girlfriends may be few and far between. What I mean by this is, REAL girlfriends that are true will always be there for you no matter what. Talking about issues you are facing, boy problems, or celebrating great things that happen in your life is an example of a true best friend. Sometimes we learn the hard way when we give much more to a friendship than the other does. This is an exercise that I think is really cool to do if you're wondering if a friend is a REAL friend. Michelle Phillips, celebrity makeup artist, life coach, and author of "Beauty Blueprint" shared this with me and I really feel it should be in every girls thoughts when dealing with friends. In an honest manner, write the traits listed on the next page under the picture or name of each of your friends. Now, decide who you will choose to be your friend. Remember, sometimes you are judged by the company you keep!

IS SHE A REAL FRIEND?

In an honest manner, write the traits listed below under the picture or name of each of your friends.

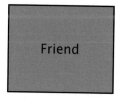

1. Smart
2. Honest
3. Fun
4. Home–body

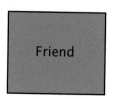

Traits of a Good Friend:
(Examples)
1. Loyal
2. Dependable
3. Truthful
4. Honest
5. Always Supportive

Traits of a Bad Friend:
(Examples)
1. Attitude Problem
2. Flaky
3. Judgemental
4. Lies
5. Undependable

Now decide, who you will choose to be your friend. Remember, sometimes you are judged by the company you keep!

BEST FRIENDS

Meghan Menasco
Best friend for four years

Nicole & Meagan Parker
Amazing best friends since the third grade

Rachel Orr
Best friend for four years
She always makes me laugh!

MAKING WISE CHOICES

What you do today, might affect the rest of our life, so check yourself... get smart and don't do something just because "all the kids are doing it." Try not to do too many stupid things. All of us make mistakes, but you must be strong and confident enough to avoid the really catastrophic bad choices. The ones marked with the skull and cross bones. You know in your heart what they are.

For instance, suppose you are at a party and a best friend asks you to try pot or ecstasy. Temptation rears its ugly head and you figure you'll try it just this once, to "see what it's like" or to "fit in" with the cool kids. Besides, your friend is going to try it and you don't want to look like a freak, so you lean toward doing it "just this once." I can't tell you the huge number of kids in rehab, who had that same thought... they gave in, JUST THIS ONCE and ended up addicted to drugs. Drugs are in the extremely bad choices column!

Drinking can kill. There are a huge number of teen deaths each year due to underage drinking. Going to a party, getting smashed, then getting in the car to either drive home or getting in the car with a friend who is drunk... will lead you down the path of a car accident that could leave you paralyzed for life or dead! Don't let the party world of alcohol ruin your life or that of a friend's... be proactive like we talked about in the beginning of the book. If you see a friend or another kid who has had too much to drink, take their car keys and get them a ride home. Maybe the next day have a talk with them about it. Be involved.

Choosing a good group of friends is one of the most important decisions you will ever make. Remember this, bad friends will most likely pull a good teenager down to their level. You don't want to be hanging out with these kinds of kids. They will get you in trouble with your family, school and maybe even the law. You need to hang out with girls that have positive attitudes, do well in school and have good relationships with their parents. Girls that understand "rules are established for a very important purpose" and that living by them will make your life head in a positive direction.

Decide what your values and morals are, then stick to them. Don't let some cute guy talk you into doing things you know are wrong and go against the grain of your values and morals. Guys will do this to you and will also lie and tell you they love you or they don't want to "go out with you" anymore if you don't have sex with them. Don't fall into the trap of some boy, just because he is cute or popular. Give yourself the right to stand up for yourself and only do what you feel comfortable doing. Maybe before you start dating, you can set up some ground rules. This way, both of you will know what to expect and if you both agree, you will avoid awkward situations. Always have pride and self-respect for yourself. Others will follow the same line of thinking, once you do!

Last, but just as important... do well in school! It is preparing you for life in the real world. After school, you are no longer a kid and you will be on your own... even in college you will be having to make decisions by yourself and take care of all your responsibilites and yes, plan to go to college. It is another wise choice for a successful life and future.

It will give you the knowledge you require for your chosen profession or career. It also gives you four years to learn about living on your own before you actually have to get a job and live completely on your own. You will learn and grow so much during your college years.

Kevin Chappell Photography

HUMILITY

You need to learn how to be humble... yet, not lose your sense of pride in yourself. This is a fine line that many girls have a problem understanding, but it is really very simple. Be proud of your achievements and popularity with people. Be proud that you have good morals and values. Be proud that you are kind, smart and successful in your endeavors.

Do not flaunt your beauty, successes, popularity or family wealth. Don't become a snob! Don't brag about yourself. Don't be a show off. Don't be pretentious and when others compliment you, always be GRACIOUS.

Compliment others about their good qualities and accomplishments. Also, learn to fix a bad situation and say I'm sorry. Don't let arguments ruin a friendship or relationship. Apologize for your part in the situation and work to fix it.

Euan Torrie ~ ET Imagez Photography

BU... THERE'S NO ONE ELSE LIKE IT!

So, now that you have found out who you are, be yourself! You are one of a kind... your best quality of all is... YOUR INDIVIDUALITY.

Develop and grow into the person you want to become and then don't let anyone try to change you. Stand your ground! Later in life you may choose a boyfriend that you date and eventually marry. Then, all of a sudden, he wants you to dress and act differently. Well, if the guy was attracted to you from the beginning, then married you... why would the Dumbo want you to change? You've got me... I don't know the answer to that.

What I do know, is that you should stay true to yourself. You decide the friends you want to hang out with and the way you want to look... how much make up to wear and the clothes that look best on you... not some anorexic movie star.

Be yourself. That is not to say you have to stay the same throughout your entire life. Two, four or six years down the road, you may want to re-invent yourself. Great! It needs to be your decision. As girls, new styles, makeup and hairdos are fun, fun, fun! We should never lose the excitement of a beautiful new look to show off at a party or get together.

On a more serious note... Being you is sometimes difficult. Sometimes it puts you in an uncomfortable situation. We are all tempted to go along with the crowd or laugh at something inappropriate. If you get into a situation where your values or morals would be radically compromised, stay true to yourself. Take the attitude that anyone who does not respect you is an idiot and does not need to be a friend or part of your life.

Learning to disassociate yourself from friends or people who want you to go down a bad path with them is sometimes tough. Especially if you like those friends. The end result of "giving in" is sometimes life altering in a very negative way.

Stay Strong! Make wise choices! Set a good example!

Be proud of who you have become. It takes tremendous effort and time to develop into a young lady that people admire and respect. Once you have achieved this goal, parents will want their young girls to be like you. You will be admired and looked up to as a fine example of today's youth. YOU will eventually be asked to be a mentor. The ultimate compliment!

"Find your sparkle, share it with someone, give others confidence to find their sparkle, don't let anyone say you can't. Go out into this world and make a splash!"

— Lauren Galley

I love giving "Girl Talks"!
This is the Cy–Hope group of amazing girls.

YOUR JOURNEY

Begin your journey with kindness. Care about others. Really listen to what our parents, teachers and friends have to say. Figure how you can spread good will throughout your school and community. Get involved! Be creative! Live your life to the fullest. Tap into your talents. You will be amazed at what can happen.

I know this seems like a lot to take in, but once you start to put my STEPS TO SUCCESS into practice, you will become the young person people admire, compliment and want their kids to emulate. You will then have become a GIRL ABOVE SOCIETY. The girl who has her life headed in a positive direction. The girl who relates well to everyone she meets. The girl who is confident about who she is... someone who always does the right thing.

Let me leave you with one last thought...
LET NO ONE COME INTO YOUR LIFE WITHOUT LEAVING A BETTER PERSON FOR HAVING KNOWN YOU!

Lauren ~

MORE INFORMATION ABOUT
GIRLS ABOVE SOCIETY

GIRLS ABOVE SOCIETY is a 501C3 organization founded by Lauren Marie Galley, an 18 year old actress/model and college honors student. This organization provides mentorship and awareness to teen girls facing the pressures of today's society. Girls Above Society is the home of "Girl Talk", a signature program lead by Lauren that builds the confidence and leadership every young girl needs to become an excellent role model in their community.

Girls Above Society
P.O. Box 130295
Spring, TX 77389
tel: 832-370-2540
website: www.girlsabovesociety.org
email: girlsabovesociety@att.net

ABOUT THE AUTHOR

Lauren Galley, Teen Mentor, Radio Host, Actress, Model and President of Girls Above Society transitioned from her high school AP program to college at age 16 embarking on a journey driven to create an anchor of empowerment for teen girls. Launching (at age 17) Girls Above Society gives Lauren the platform of teen to teen mentorship combined with film visuals creating a social media movement.

As a voice to young teen girls, Lauren hosts her own radio show "The Lauren Galley Show" on her CETV Channel & Blogtalkradio. She has been featured on Fox News, Teen Vogue, Best Ever You Radio, and Talented Teens in the UK. Her writings have appeared in numerous publications such as International Talent Magazine, Smart Girls Guide, Babble, and The Huffington Post covering issues of the many pressures young teens are facing in today's society.

Lauren's serves as Youth Advocate for Free2Luv airing her Free2BeYOU Series, and as Teen Commentator for Houston Family Magazine as well as representing the Best Ever You Community as Chief Teen Advisor. Lauren enjoys traveling throughout the U.S. giving her signature "Girl Talks."

Made in the USA
San Bernardino, CA
25 September 2015